ART & WONDER

An Illustrated Anthology of Visionary Poetry

Selected and Introduced by Kate Farrell

The Metropolitan Museum of Art · New York
A Bulfinch Press Book/Little, Brown and Company
Boston · New York · Toronto · London

Front jacket: *Autumn Grasses* (detail)
Shibata Zeshin, Japanese, 1807–1891
Panel from a two-fold screen; ink,
lacquer, and silver leaf on paper
Gift of A. W. Bahr, 1958 58.547.26

Back jacket: *Unicorns (Legend—Sea Calm)*
Arthur B. Davies, American, 1862–1928
Oil on canvas, ca. 1906
Bequest of Lillie P. Bliss, 1931 31.67.12

Endpapers: Detail from a hand-colored woodblock print
by Michael Ostendorfer, German, 1519–1559
From *Astronomicum Caesareum* (Imperial Astronomy)
by Petrus Apianus, German, 1501–1552
Ingoldstadt, Bavaria, May 1540
Gift of Herbert N. Straus, 1925 25.17

Page 1: *Spanish Fountain*
John Singer Sargent, American, 1856–1925
Watercolor and graphite on white wove paper
Purchase, Joseph Pulitzer Bequest, 1915 15.142.6

I especially thank Mary Beth Brewer, my editor in the
Department of Special Publications, whose meticulous good
judgment was a vital part of the book's creation. Thanks also
to Cathy Hansen who guided its production, Tina Fjotland
who designed it so beautifully, and Ilana Goldberg who
capably managed numerous details.

Kate Farrell

For acknowledgments of the use of other
copyrighted material, see page 138.

Compilation and introduction copyright
© 1996 by Kate Farrell
Illustrations copyright
© 1996 by The Metropolitan Museum of Art

Unless otherwise noted, translations are by Kate Farrell.

First Edition
First Printing

ISBN 0-87099-813-7 (MMA)
ISBN 0-8212-2328-3 (Bulfinch Press—distributor)
Library of Congress Catalog Card Number: 96-76453

Published by
The Metropolitan Museum of Art, New York,
and Bulfinch Press
Bulfinch Press is an imprint and trademark of
Little, Brown and Company (Inc.)
Published simultaneously in Canada by
Little, Brown & Company (Canada) Limited

Produced by the
Department of Special Publications,
The Metropolitan Museum of Art
Designed by Tina Fjotland
Photography on pages 7, 8, 17, 20, 74, 82, 92,
and 120 by Malcolm Varon, N.Y.; on pages 14,
105, and 112 by Schecter Lee
All other photography by The Metropolitan
Museum of Art Photograph Studio

Printed in Singapore

I am certain of nothing but the holiness of the heart's affections and the truth of imagination.

JOHN KEATS

CONTENTS

INTRODUCTION

"I dwell in Possibility," wrote Emily Dickinson, summing up the magic of inspiration in a poem that has since lifted countless readers into her poetic paradise. Thus have poets through the ages shared with those in other times and places visions of realms beyond ordinary existence. This collection, which unites visionary poems from all over the world with works of art from the Metropolitan Museum, seemed an exciting way to invite readers to dwell more deeply in the enchanted scenery of poetic possibility.

The book holds many kinds of poetic visions—from light-hearted fantasies to sublime revelations, with all sorts of outlooks and inspirations—and is divided into four sections. *Dwelling in Possibility* contains poems of hope and longing; *Sailing to Byzantium*, poetic reveries and dream poems. In *The Secrets of the World* are poems of artistic and spiritual struggle and epiphany, and *A Further Sea* offers glimpses of paradise, terrestrial and celestial.

To better reflect the imaginative richness of the poems, most are matched with two works of art. The art works illuminate separate aspects of the poem, unfolding its movement from mood to mood or moment to moment or otherwise animating its drama and mystery. Sometimes there is the added interaction of a second related poem, and some poems appear with a single work of art. Overall, I looked for works and combinations that provided an evocative flow of art and poetry and a lively interplay between words and images.

The great visionary poet and artist William Blake said that poetry and art were ways to converse with paradise. In bringing poetry's hopes and heavens to visual life with art, I hoped to condense into these pages some of the immense scope and beauty of that miraculous conversation, in which the invisible becomes visible and the impossible, possible.

Kate Farrell

Morning on the Seine near Giverny (detail)
Claude Monet, French, 1840–1926
Oil on canvas, 1897

Dwelling in Possibility

Girl at a Window
Balthus (Balthasar Klossowski),
French, b. 1908
Oil on canvas, 1957

I Dwell in Possibility

I dwell in Possibility –
A fairer House than Prose –
More numerous of Windows –
Superior – for Doors –

Of Chambers as the Cedars –
Impregnable of Eye –
And for an Everlasting Roof
The Gambrels of the Sky –

Of Visitors – the fairest –
For occupation – This –
The spreading wide my narrow Hands
To gather Paradise –

EMILY DICKINSON, American, 1830–1886

Oriental Pleasure Garden (detail)
Paul Klee, German, 1879–1940
Oil on cardboard, 1925

I Wish I Might Find a Cave

FROM HIPPOLYTOS

I wish I might find a cave
secret beneath the cliffs
where a god would change me to bird—
then I would fly with the flocks
far, far away where the sea breaks
on Adriatic shores,
where the blue Eridanus empties
and the daughters of the Sun
as their father descends beneath the waves
sprinkle those dark-glinting waters
with tears from their amber eyes
in sorrow for Phaëthon.

I would fly to the coast of apples
of which many tales are told,
the far Hesperian shore
where the mighty Lord of ocean
forbids all further voyaging
and marks the sacred limits
of heaven, which Atlas holds.
There the immortal streams
flow fresh by the couch of God
where he lies with his lovely ones—
and earth, the mother of life, yields up
blessings of harvest to enrich
a bliss that never ends.

EURIPIDES, Greek, ca. 484–406 B.C.
(Translated by Frederick Morgan)

Perseus Rescuing Andromeda
Detail of a fresco from the
Imperial Villa at Boscotrecase
Roman, last decade of the 1st century B.C.

The Bathing Pool (detail)
Hubert Robert,
French, 1733–1808
Oil on canvas

The Song of Wandering Aengus

I went out to the hazel wood,
Because a fire was in my head,
And cut and peeled a hazel wand,
And hooked a berry to a thread;
And when white moths were on the wing,
And moth-like stars were flickering out,
I dropped the berry in a stream
And caught a little silver trout.

When I had laid it on the floor
I went to blow the fire aflame,
But something rustled on the floor,
And someone called me by my name:
It had become a glimmering girl
With apple blossom in her hair
Who called me by my name and ran
And faded through the brightening air.

Though I am old with wandering
Through hollow lands and hilly lands,
I will find out where she has gone,
And kiss her lips and take her hands;
And walk among long dappled grass,
And pluck till time and times are done
The silver apples of the moon,
The golden apples of the sun.

WILLIAM BUTLER YEATS, Irish, 1865–1939

The Aegean Sea (detail)
Frederick Edwin Church,
American, 1826–1900
Oil on canvas

The Storm
Pierre-Auguste Cot,
French, 1837–1883
Oil on canvas, 1880

Marine
Salomon van Ruysdael, Dutch, 1600/1603–1670
Oil on wood, 1650

The Most Beautiful

I.
But the most beautiful of all is the Un-Found Island:
the one that the King of Spain received from
    his cousin
the King of Portugal with a royal seal
and a papal edict in Gothic Latin.

The Prince set sail for the fabulous kingdom,
he saw the Fortunate Islands: Iunonia, Gorgo, Hera
and the Sargasso Sea and the Secret Sea
while looking for the island . . . But the island
    wasn't there.

In vain the galleons with bulging bellies and
    billowing sails,
in vain the sleek, newly-equipped caravels:
after the papal decree, the island disappeared,
and Portugal and Spain are still searching.

II.
The Island exists. It appears sometimes in the distance
between Tenerife and Palma, veiled in mystery:
". . . the Un-Found Island!" The wise old Canaryman
points it out to the foreigner from the high peak of Teide.

Ancient pirate maps show it:
. . . Island of—Finding? . . . Wandering Island? . . .
It is the magic island that slips through the seas;
now and then the navigators see her nearby . . .

Their prows almost brush that blissful shore:
towering palms sway amid flowers never seen before,
fragrance drifts from the lush, heavenly forest,
the cardamom weeps, the rubber trees ooze . . .

She is announced, like a courtesan, by her perfume,
the Un-Found Island . . . But, if the pilot steers her way,
she quickly vanishes like a fantastic apparition,
tinting herself with the blue color of the faraway . . .

GUIDO GOZZANO, Italian, 1883–1916

Allegory (detail)
Charles Prendergast, American, 1863–1948
Watercolor over pencil, ca. 1927–28

Song

That tree with trembling leaves
is longing for something.

That tree, so lovely to look at,
seems to want to give away flowers:
it is longing for something.

That tree, so lovely to see,
seems to want to flower:
it is longing for something.

It seems to want to give away flowers:
they are already showing; come and look at them:
it is longing for something.

It seems to want to flower:
they are already showing; come and see them:
it is longing for something.

They are already showing; come and look at them.
Let the women come to pick the fruit:
it is longing for something.

DIEGO HURTADO DE MENDOZA, Spanish, 1364–1404

Amour
Cover for a suite of twelve lithographs
Maurice Denis, French, 1870–1943
Color lithograph, ca. 1899

Spring Blossoms, Montclair, New Jersey (detail)
George Inness, American, 1824–1894
Oil and crayon or charcoal on canvas

17

The Natchez
Eugène Delacroix, French,
1798–1863
Oil on canvas

The Child Is Introduced to the Cosmos at Birth

Ho! Ye Sun, Moon, Stars, all ye that move in
    the heavens,
       I bid you hear me!
Into your midst has come a new life.
      Consent ye, I implore!
Make its path smooth, that it may reach
    the brow of the first hill!

Ho! Ye Winds, Clouds, Rain, Mist, all ye
    that move in the air,
       I bid you hear me!
Into your midst has come a new life.
      Consent ye, I implore!
Make its path smooth, that it may reach
    the brow of the second hill!

Ho! Ye Hills, Valleys, Rivers, Lakes, Trees,
　　Grasses, all ye of the earth,
　　　　I bid you hear me!
Into your midst has come a new life.
　　Consent ye, I implore!
Make its path smooth, that it may reach
　　the brow of the third hill!

Ho! Ye Birds, great and small, that fly in the air,
Ho! Ye Animals, great and small, that dwell
　　in the forest,
Ho! Ye insects that creep among the grasses
　　and burrow in the ground:
　　　　I bid you hear me!
Into your midst has come a new life.
　　Consent ye, I implore!
Make its path smooth, that it may reach the
　　brow of the fourth hill!

Ho! All ye of the heavens, all ye of the air,
　　all ye of the earth:
　　　　I bid you all to hear me!
Into your midst has come a new life.
　　Consent ye, consent ye all, I implore!
Make its path smooth—then shall it travel
　　beyond the four hills.

ANONYMOUS, OMAHA INDIAN
　　(Translated by Alice Fletcher)

The Song of the Waters
Jerome Thompson, American, 1814–1886
Oil on canvas, 1878

Sensation

On blue summer evenings I'll go
    down the pathways
Pricked by the grain, crushing the
    tender grass—
Dreaming, I'll feel its coolness on
    my feet.
I'll let the wind bathe my bare head.

I won't talk at all, I won't think
    about anything
But infinite love will rise in my soul,
And I'll go far, very far, like a gypsy
Into nature—happy, as if with
    a woman.

ARTHUR RIMBAUD, French, 1854–1891
(Translated by Kenneth Koch)

Cypresses; Wheat Field with Cypresses
Vincent van Gogh, Dutch, 1853–1890
Oil on canvas

The Song Turning Back Into Itself 7

the fly-away song

Get that feeling sometimes
that
you-cant-hold-me-down
feeling

Wanna shatter
into
ten thousand fragments of emotion—

Splinter!

Rise
above this quivering concrete world
& go sailing thru beds & minds

Sail
higher
&
HIGHER

Crazy that way
SING
one sweet long song to undo
all sickness & suffering
down there on the ground . . .
one huge human gust of insight
& forgiveness

SOARING
over rooftops with
Chagall's chickens

ALIVE

WAKING!

AL YOUNG, American, b. 1939

Daily News
Dona Nelson, American, b. 1952
Oil on canvas, 1983

View of San Francisco, Number 2
Peter Saul, American, b. 1934
Oil and acrylic on canvas, 1988

Floating Bridges

Oh what tremendous multitudes,
invisible and ever-changing,
come to this garden
and linger forever!

Every step we take on Earth
takes us to a new world.
Every single footstep
lands on a floating bridge.

I know that there is no such thing
as a straight road.
Only a vast labyrinth
of intricate crossroads.

Our steps incessantly
create as we go
immense spirals
of unfolding pathways.

Oh garden of fresh
possibilities! Oh garden
of all I still am not
but could and should have been!

FEDERICO GARCÍA LORCA, Spanish, 1899–1936

The Months of the Year
Detail from an embroidered picture
English, second quarter of the 17th century
Wool, silk, silver thread, and purl on canvas

Mural from the Temple of Longing ⟍ Thither ⟋
Paul Klee, German, 1879–1940
Watercolor and transferred printing ink on gesso on fabric, 1922

The Archangel Gabriel
One of two panels, representing *The Annunciation,*
from a polyptych
Gerard David, Netherlandish, active by 1484, d. 1523
Oil on wood

On Angels

All was taken away from you: white dresses,
wings, even existence.
Yet I believe you,
messengers.

There, where the world is turned inside out,
a heavy fabric embroidered with stars and beasts,
you stroll, inspecting the trustworthy seams.

Short is your stay here:
now and then at a matinal hour, if the sky is clear
in a melody repeated by a bird,
or in the smell of apples at the close of day
when the light makes the orchards magic.

They say somebody has invented you
but to me this does not sound convincing
for humans invented themselves as well.

The voice—no doubt it is a valid proof,
as it can belong only to radiant creatures
weightless and winged (after all, why not?),
girdled with the lightning.

I have heard that voice many a time when asleep
and, what is strange, I understood more or less
an order or an appeal in an unearthly tongue:

day draws near
another one
do what you can.

CZESLAW MILOSZ, Polish, b. 1911
(Translated by Czeslaw Milosz)

Envying Tobias

No more do we
Of angels talk;
'Tis no more of any read

That an angel came
With us to walk,
And to a woman said

— Blessed be thou,
To thee I bow
My wise and lovely head—

I need an angel,
Such as young
Tobias met:

Now do, to me,
God, my dear,
Send quickly here

That angel, which shall be
Teacher to Thine own every son,
And bring this son to Thee.

JAMES STEPHENS, Irish, 1882–1950

The Archangel Raphael and Tobias
Neri di Bicci, Italian (Florentine), 1419–1491
Tempera and gold on wood

A Message from the Crane

On a deserted islet in
    the ocean
Stay even if the sun sets and
    the moon
Stay even if winds howl
    and rain.

During the day chitchat
    with waves
At night repeat the names
    of stars
Memorize the names of
    countless stars

Eat grass berries
Wet your throat with
    dewdrops

Weave your dress
    with flowers
Inscribe your syllables on
    the sand

Girl Viewing Plum Blossoms by Lantern Light
Suzuki Harunobu, Japanese, 1725–1770
Polychrome woodblock print, ca. 1768

Wait there
On that lonely island.

Don't say my words
    are foolish
The words I send to the winds.

Flying over the six oceans
I'll bring you back

The joy
Of wings growing in
    my armpits
Of my flesh and bones

Till that day that morning
Wait.

PAK FU-JIN, Korean, b. 1916
    (Translated by Peter H. Lee)

Minowa, Kanasugi, Mikawashima
Utagawa Hiroshige, Japanese, 1797–1858
Woodblock print in colors from the series
One Hundred Famous Views of Edo, 1857

Entrance to a Garden
Paul Cézanne, French, 1839–1906
Watercolor over pencil on cream-colored paper

Sometimes

When I take your hand
It is like a door, opening . . .

A garden . . .
A road leading out through a
    Mediterranean landscape . . .

Finally: a smell of salt,
the port,
A ship leaving for strange and
    distant countries.

THOMAS MCGRATH, American, 1916–1990

View of the Port of Marseilles (detail)
Paul Signac, French, 1863–1935
Oil on canvas, 1905

Sailing to Byzantium

Sailing to Byzantium

Medallion of St. John the Baptist
One of the nine surviving
Djumati medallions from an icon frame
Byzantine, early 12th century
Gold, cloisonné enamel

1.

That is no country for old men. The young
In one another's arms, birds in the trees
—Those dying generations—at their song,
The salmon-falls, the mackerel-crowded seas,
Fish, flesh, or fowl, commend all summer long
Whatever is begotten, born, and dies.
Caught in that sensual music all neglect
Monuments of unaging intellect.

2.

An aged man is but a paltry thing,
A tattered coat upon a stick, unless
Soul clap its hands and sing, and louder sing
For every tatter in its mortal dress,
Nor is there singing school but studying
Monuments of its own magnificence;
And therefore I have sailed the seas and come
To the holy city of Byzantium.

3.

O sages standing in God's holy fire
As in the gold mosaic of a wall,
Come from the holy fire, perne in a gyre,
And be the singing-masters of my soul.
Consume my heart away; sick with desire
And fastened to a dying animal
It knows not what it is; and gather me
Into the artifice of eternity.

4.

Once out of nature I shall never take
My bodily form from any natural thing,
But such a form as Grecian goldsmiths make
Of hammered gold and gold enameling
To keep a drowsy Emperor awake;
Or set upon a golden bough to sing
To lords and ladies of Byzantium
Of what is past, or passing, or to come.

WILLIAM BUTLER YEATS, Irish, 1865–1939

The Grand Canal, Venice (detail)
Joseph Mallord William Turner, British, 1775–1851
Oil on canvas

Royalty

One beautiful morning, in a land of very gentle
people, a splendid man and woman announced
in a public place: "My friends, I want her
to be queen!" "I want to be queen!" She laughed
and trembled. He spoke of a revelation, of a trial
ended. They sank into one another's arms.

In fact, they were monarchs for one whole morning,
in which crimson banners hung from the houses,
and all that afternoon, in which they
made their way toward the gardens of palms.

ARTHUR RIMBAUD, French, 1854–1891

Invisible Particles of Air

Invisible particles of air
flutter and flame around me;
the sky dissolves in gold flashes;
the earth trembles with happiness;
I hear murmuring kisses and flapping wings
floating on waves of harmony;
my eyes close. . . .What is happening?
—Love is passing by!

GUSTAVO ADOLF BÉCQUER, Spanish, 1836–1870

Venus and Adonis
Detail from a set of mythological subjects after Raphael
French, Paris; designed 1684–86 by François Bonnemer
(French, 1638–1689) and Pierre de Sève the Younger
(French, ca. 1623–1695)
Woven 1686–92 at the Gobelins Manufactory of Louis XIV
Wool, silk, and silver thread

Playing Cards
(three from a set of fifty-two)
South Lowlands, Burgundian Territories,
probably Flanders, 1475–85
Ink, tempera, and metal foil on pasteboard

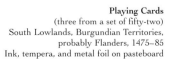

Elevation

Above the ponds, above the valleys,
The mountains, the woods, the clouds, the seas;
Beyond the sun, beyond the ether,
Beyond the borders of the starry spheres,

My spirit, you move so deftly,
And, like a good swimmer revelling in the sea,
You surge joyfully through deep immensity
With virile, inexpressible pleasure.

Fly far away from this unhealthy air
And bathe yourself in a higher atmosphere;
Drink like a potion, pure and divine,
The lucid fire that fills cosmic emptiness.

After the troubles and vast sadness
Which thicken the fog that darkens existence,
Happy the one who has strong enough wings
To soar toward lands, bright and serene!

The one whose thoughts are like larks,
Freely rising into morning skies,
Glides above life and understands effortlessly
The language of flowers and all voiceless things!

CHARLES BAUDELAIRE, French, 1821–1867

Icarus (Icare)
Henri Matisse, French, 1869–1954
Pochoir (color stencil) from *Jazz*,
published by Tériade, Paris, 1947

Landscape with Stars (detail)
Henri-Edmond Cross, French, 1856–1910
Watercolor

Kubla Khan

In Xanadu did Kubla Khan
A stately pleasure-dome decree:
Where Alph, the sacred river, ran
Through caverns measureless to man
    Down to a sunless sea.
So twice five miles of fertile ground
With walls and towers were girdled round:
And here were gardens bright with sinuous rills,
Where blossomed many an incense-bearing tree;
And here were forests ancient as the hills,
Enfolding sunny spots of greenery.

But oh! that deep romantic chasm which slanted
Down the green hill athwart a cedarn cover!
A savage place! as holy and enchanted
As e'er beneath a waning moon was haunted
By woman wailing for her demon-lover!
And from this chasm, with ceaseless turmoil seething
As if this earth in fast thick pants were breathing,
A mighty fountain momently was forced:
Amid whose swift half-intermitted burst
Huge fragments vaulted like rebounding hail
Or chaffy grain beneath the thresher's flail:
And 'mid these dancing rocks at once and ever
It flung up momently the sacred river.
Five miles meandering with a mazy motion
Through wood and dale the sacred river ran,
Then reached the caverns measureless to man,
And sank in tumult to a lifeless ocean:

And 'mid this tumult Kubla heard from far
Ancestral voices prophesying war!
    The shadow of the dome of pleasure
    Floated midway on the waves;
    Where was heard the mingled measure
    From the fountain and the caves.
It was a miracle of rare device,
A sunny pleasure-dome with caves of ice!

A damsel with a dulcimer
In a vision once I saw:
    It was an Abyssinian maid,
    And on her dulcimer she played,
    Singing of Mount Abora.
    Could I revive within me
    Her symphony and song,
    To such a deep delight 'twould win me,
That with music loud and long,
I would build that dome in air,
That sunny dome! those caves of ice!
And all who heard should see them there,
And all should cry, Beware! Beware!
His flashing eyes, his floating hair!
Weave a circle round him thrice,
And close your eyes with holy dread,
For he on honey-dew hath fed,
And drunk the milk of Paradise.

SAMUEL TAYLOR COLERIDGE, English, 1772–1834

The Concert
Detail from a tapestry
English (London), ca. 1690–1715
Wool and silk

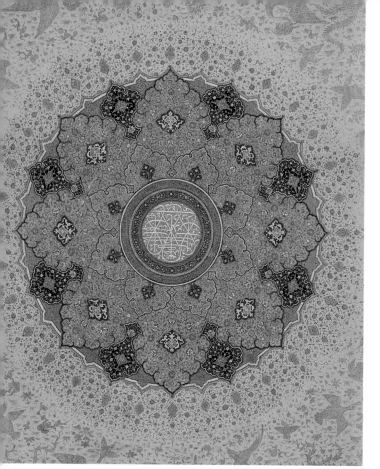

The Borderland–9

I saw, in the twilight of flagging
    consciousness,
My body floating down an ink-black
    stream
With its mass of feelings, with its
    varied emotion,
With its many-coloured lifelong store
    of memories,
With its flutesong. And as it drifted on
    and on
Its outlines dimmed; and among familiar
    tree-shaded
Villages on the banks, the sounds of
    evening
Worship grew faint, doors were closed,
    lamps
Were covered, boats were moored to the
    ghāts. Crossings
From either side of the stream stopped;
    night thickened;
From the forest-branches fading
    birdsong offered
Self-sacrifice to a huge silence.
Dark formlessness settled over all
    diversity
Of land and water. As shadow, as particles,
    my body
Fused with endless night. I came to rest
At the altar of the stars. Alone, amazed,
    I stared
Upwards with hands clasped and said:
    "Sun, you have removed
Your rays: show now your loveliest,
    kindliest form
That I may see the Person who dwells in
    me as in you."

RABINDRANATH TAGORE, Indian, 1861–1941
(Translated by William Radice)

Untitled
Jerry Uelsmann, American, b. 1934
Gelatin silver print, 1980, from 1976 negative

Adagio

Third Movement from "Holiday Music in the Evening"

A dream gives what the day wore out;
At night, when the conscious will surrenders,
Some powers, set free, reach upward,
Sensing something godly, and following.
The woods rustle, and the stream, and through
    the night blue sky
Of the quick soul, the summer lightning blows.
The world and my self, everything
Within and without me, grows into one.
Clouds drift through my heart,
Woods dream my dream,
House and pear tree tell me
The forgotten story of common childhood.
Streams resound and gorges cast shadows in me,
The moon, and the faint star, my close friends.
But the mild night,
That bows with its gentle clouds above me,
Has my mother's face,
Kisses me, smiling, with inexhaustible love,
Shakes her head dreamily
As she used to do, and her hair
Waves through the world, and within it
The thousand stars, shuddering, turn pale.

HERMANN HESSE, German, 1877–1962
    (Translated by James Wright)

Glowing Night
Oscar Bluemner, American, 1867–1938
Watercolor and pencil on paper

When, With You Asleep

When, with you asleep, I plunge into
    your soul,
and I listen, with my ear
on your naked breast,
to your tranquil heart, it seems to me
that, in its deep throbbing, I surprise
the secret of the center
of the world.

    It seems to me
that legions of angels
on celestial steeds
—as when, in the height
of the night we listen, without a breath
and our ears to the earth,
to distant hoofbeats that never arrive—,
that legions of angels
are coming through you, from afar
—like the Three Kings
to the eternal birth
of our love—,
they are coming through you, from afar,
to bring me, in your dreams,
the secret of the center
of the heavens.

JUAN RAMÓN JIMÉNEZ, Spanish, 1881–1958
    (Translated by Perry Higman)

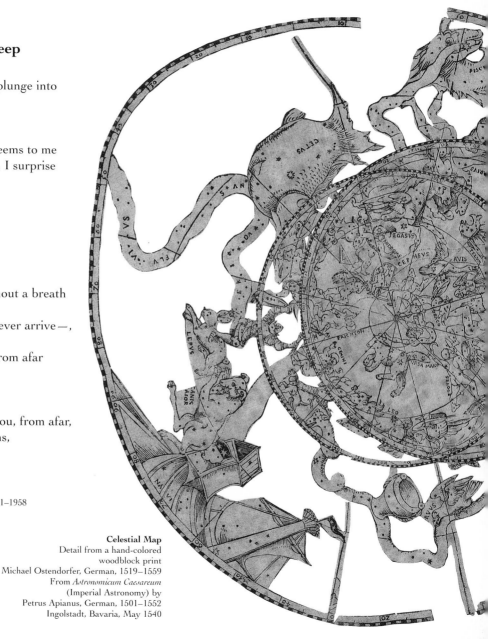

Celestial Map
Detail from a hand-colored
woodblock print
Michael Ostendorfer, German, 1519–1559
From *Astronomicum Caesareum*
(Imperial Astronomy) by
Petrus Apianus, German, 1501–1552
Ingolstadt, Bavaria, May 1540

The Lovers (detail)
Marc Chagall, French (b. Russia),
1887–1985
Oil on canvas, 1913–14

A Maid Asleep
Johannes Vermeer, Dutch, 1632–1675
Oil on canvas

Our Life Is Twofold

From The Dream

Our life is twofold: Sleep hath its own world,
A boundary between the things misnamed
Death and existence: Sleep hath its own world,
And a wide realm of wild reality.
And dreams in their development have breath,
And tears, and tortures, and the touch of joy;
They leave a weight upon our waking thoughts,
They take a weight from off our waking toils,
They do divide our being; they become
A portion of ourselves as of our time,
And look like heralds of eternity;
They pass like spirits of the past,—they speak
Like sibyls of the future; they have power—
The tyranny of pleasure and of pain:
They make us what we were not—what they will,
And shake us with the vision that's gone by,
The dread of vanished shadows—are they so?
Is not the past all shadow?—What are they?
Creations of the mind? The mind can make
Substance, and people planets of its own
With beings brighter than have been, and give
A breath to forms which can outlive all flesh.

Lord Byron, English, 1788–1824

Sonnet XLIII

When most I wink, then do mine eyes best see,
For all the day they view things unrespected;
But when I sleep, in dreams they look on thee,
And, darkly bright, are bright in dark directed.
Then thou, whose shadow shadows doth make bright,
How would thy shadow's form form happy show
To the clear day with thy much clearer light,
When to unseeing eyes thy shade shines so!
How would, I say, mine eyes be blessèd made
By looking on thee in the living day,
When in dead night thy fair imperfect shade
Through heavy sleep on sightless eyes doth stay!
    All days are nights to see till I see thee,
    And nights bright days when dreams do show thee me.

WILLIAM SHAKESPEARE, English, 1564–1616

Sleeping Muse
Constantin Brancusi,
French (b. Rumania), 1876–1957
Bronze, 1910

Sleeping in the Forest

I thought the earth
remembered me, she
took me back so tenderly, arranging
her dark skirts, her pockets
full of lichens and seeds. I slept
as never before, a stone
on the riverbed, nothing
between me and the white fire of the stars
but my thoughts, and they floated
light as moths among the branches
of the perfect trees. All night
I heard the small kingdoms breathing
around me, the insects, and the birds
who do their work in the darkness. All night
I rose and fell, as if in water, grappling
with a luminous doom. By morning
I had vanished at least a dozen times
into something better.

MARY OLIVER, American, b. 1935

Emergence

If you have watched a moulting mantis
With exquisite precision and no less
Exquisite patience, extricate itself
Leaf-green and like a green leaf clinging
Little by little, leg by leg
Out of its chiton shell, you likewise know
How one day coaxes itself out of another
Slowly, slowly by imperceptible degrees
Of gray, and having fully emerged, pauses
To dry its wings.

ROBERT FRANCIS, American, 1901–1987

Cherry Tree Beside a Waterfall
Japanese, late 18th century
Exterior of a writing box cover,
sprinkled gold on lacquer

Hanging Vase and Praying Mantis (detail)
Japanese, 19th century
Exterior of a writing box cover;
sprinkled gold, inlay of
mother of pearl and lead,
aventurine on black lacquer

Imaginary Daylight

At night above my bed
The shadows of the shutters
Float on the ceiling
And, through the slats, leaves shiver
In the breeze from the river
As the streetlamp glow
Dissolves all the floors
Of the building above me,

Illumining a country
Of gardens, arbors, fountains
Where people talk about momentous things
With perfect kindness and quiet certainty,
And I am the grubworm who sleeps in the soil
Beneath the beautiful paths
Where they are thinking and walking.

KATE FARRELL, American, b. 1946

Rumors from an Aeolian Harp

There is a vale which none hath seen,
Where foot of man has never been,
Such as here lives with toil and strife,
An anxious and a sinful life.

There every virtue has its birth,
Ere it descends upon the earth,
And thither every deed returns,
Which in the generous bosom burns.

There love is warm, and youth is young,
And poetry is yet unsung,
For Virtue still adventures there,
And freely breathes her native air.

And ever, if you hearken well,
You still may hear its vesper bell,
And tread of high-souled men go by,
Their thoughts conversing with the sky.

HENRY DAVID THOREAU, American, 1817–1862

Seated Harp Player
Cycladic, 3rd millennium B.C.
Marble

Sun
Detail from a hand-colored woodblock print
Michael Ostendorfer, German, 1519–1559
From *Astronomicum Caesareum* (Imperial Astronomy)
by Petrus Apianus, German, 1501–1552
Ingolstadt, Bavaria, May 1540

The Brave Man

The sun, that brave man,
Comes through boughs that lie in wait,
That brave man.

Green and gloomy eyes
In dark forms of the grass
Run away.

The good stars,
Pale helms and spiky spurs,
Run away.

Fears of my bed,
Fears of life and fears of death,
Run away.

That brave man comes up
From below and walks without mediation,
That brave man.

WALLACE STEVENS, American, 1879–1955

Day-Blind

One clap of day and the dream
rushes back
where it came from. For a moment
the ground is still moist with it.
Then day settles. You step onto dry land.

Morning picks out the four
corners, coffeepot, shawl of dust
on a cupboard. Stunned
by brightness, that dream—
where did it go?

All day you grope in a web
of invisible stars. The day sky soaks them up
like dreams. If you could see
in the light, you'd see what fires
keep spinning, spinning their mesh of threads

around you. They're closer
than you think, pulsing
into the blue. You press your forehead
to the cool glass.

They must be out there in all that dazzle.

CHANA BLOCH, American, b. 1939

From Williamsburg Bridge
Edward Hopper, American, 1882–1967
Oil on canvas, 1928

Strawberry Thief
Detail from a printed cotton, registered 1883
William Morris, British, 1834–1896
Printed by Morris and Co., Merton Abbey

Steers at Play (detail)
Lawrence H. Lebduska, American, 1894–1966
Oil on canvas, 1937

The Waking

I strolled across
An open field;
The sun was out;
Heat was happy.

This way! This way!
The wren's throat shimmered,
Either to other,
The blossoms sang.

The stones sang,
The little ones did,
And flowers jumped
Like small goats.

A ragged fringe
Of daisies waved;
I wasn't alone
In a grove of apples.

Far in the wood
A nestling sighed;
The dew loosened
Its morning smells.

I came where the river
Ran over stones:
My ears knew
An early joy.

And all the waters
Of all the streams
Sang in my veins
That summer day.

THEODORE ROETHKE, American, 1908–1963

Why the Face of the Clock
Is Not Truly a Circle

Time is not gone,
Time does not go,
Time can be found again
Old men know
If you travel a journey.

Paris again
And that scent in the air,
That sound in the street,
And the time is still there
At the end of the journey.

Turn at the door
Climb the stone stair —
What fragrance is that
In the dark, on the air,
At the end of the journey?

Time does not go:
Time keeps its place.
But oh the brown hair
And oh the bright face!
Where? By what journey?

ARCHIBALD MacLEISH, American, 1892–1982

Young Woman Seated on a Sofa
Berthe Morisot, French, 1841–1895
Oil on canvas

The Garden of the Tuileries on a Winter Afternoon (detail)
Camille Pissarro, French, 1830–1903
Oil on canvas, 1899

Before the Beginning of Years

FROM ATALANTA IN CALYDON

Before the beginning of years
    There came to the making of man
Time, with a gift of tears;
    Grief, with a glass that ran;
Pleasure, with pain for leaven;
    Summer, with flowers that fell;
Remembrance fallen from heaven,
    And madness risen from hell;
Strength without hands to smite;
    Love that endures for a breath;

Night, the shadow of light,
    And life, the shadow of death.
And the high gods took in hand
    Fire, and the falling of tears,
And a measure of sliding sand
    From under the feet of the years;
And froth and drift of the sea;
    And dust of the laboring earth;
And bodies of things to be
    In the houses of death and of birth;
And wrought with weeping and laughter,
    And fashioned with loathing and love,

With life before and after
    And death beneath and above,
For a day and a night and a morrow,
    That his strength might endure for a span
With travail and heavy sorrow,
    The holy spirit of man.
From the winds of the north and the south
    They gathered as unto strife;
They breathed upon his mouth,
    They filled his body with life;
Eyesight and speech they wrought
    For the veils of the soil therein,
A time for labor and thought,
    A time to serve and to sin;
They gave him light in his ways,
    And love, and a space for delight,
And beauty and length of days,
    And night, and sleep in the night,
His speech is a burning fire;
    With his lips he travaileth;
In his heart is a blind desire,
    In his eyes foreknowledge of death;
He weaves, and is clothed with derision;
    Sows, and he shall not reap;
His life is a watch or a vision
    Between a sleep and a sleep.

ALGERNON CHARLES SWINBURNE, English, 1837–1909

The Chariot of Apollo; Pandora
Odilon Redon, French, 1840–1916
Oil on canvas

The Angels

They all have tired mouths
and bright seamless souls.
And a longing (as for sin)
sometimes haunts their dream.

They are almost all alike;
in God's gardens they keep still,
like many, many intervals
in his might and melody.

Only when they spread their wings
are they wakers of a wind:
as if God with his broad sculptor-
hands leafed through the pages
in the dark book of the beginning.

RAINER MARIA RILKE, Austrian, 1875–1926
(Translated by Edward Snow)

The Archangel Gabriel with Heavenly Host (detail)
One of two leaves representing
The Annunciation, from a Book of Hours
French (Paris), 1465
Possibly Jean de Laval
Tempera, ink, and gold leaf on vellum

Angels
Detail from *The Adoration of the Shepherds*
Marcellus Coffermans,
Netherlandish, active 1549–1570
Oil on wood

An Altogether Different Language

There was a church in Umbria, Little Portion,
Already old eight hundred years ago.
It was abandoned and in disrepair
But it was called St. Mary of the Angels
For it was known to be the haunt of angels,
Often at night the country people
Could hear them singing there.

What was it like, to listen to the angels,
To hear those mountain-fresh, those simple voices
Poured out on the bare stones of Little Portion
In hymns of joy?
No one has told us.
Perhaps it needs another language
That we have still to learn,
An altogether different language.

ANNE PORTER, American, b. 1911

A Vision

In the Nine Provinces there is not room enough:
I want to soar high among the clouds,
And, far beyond the Eight Limits of the compass,
Cast my gaze across the unmeasured void.
I will wear as my gown the red mists of sunrise,
And as my skirt the white fringes of the clouds:
My canopy—the dim lustre of Space:
My chariot—six dragons mounting heavenward:
And before the light of Time has shifted a pace
Suddenly stand upon the World's blue rim.
       The doors of Heaven swing open,
The double gates shine with a red light.
I roam and linger in the palace of Wēn-ch'ang,
I climb up to the hall of T'ai-wei.
The Lord God lies at his western lattice:
And the lesser Spirits are together in the eastern gallery.
They wash me in a bath of rainbow-spray
And gird me with a belt of jasper and rubies.
I wander at my ease gathering divine herbs:
I bend down and touch the scented flowers.
Wang-tzǔ gives me drugs of long-life
And Hsien-mēn hands me strange potions.
By the partaking of food I evade the rites of Death:
My span is extended to the enjoyment of life everlasting.

Ts-ao Chih, Chinese, 192–232
    (Translated by Arthur Waley)

The Palace of Nine Perfections
Detail from a set of twelve hanging scrolls
Yüan Chiang, active ca. 1690–1746,
Chinese, Ch'ing dynasty
Ink and color on silk, dated 1691

Lohan
Detail from a handscroll,
The Sixteen Lohans
Wu Pin, active ca. 1583–1626,
Chinese, Ming dynasty
Ink and color on paper, dated 1591

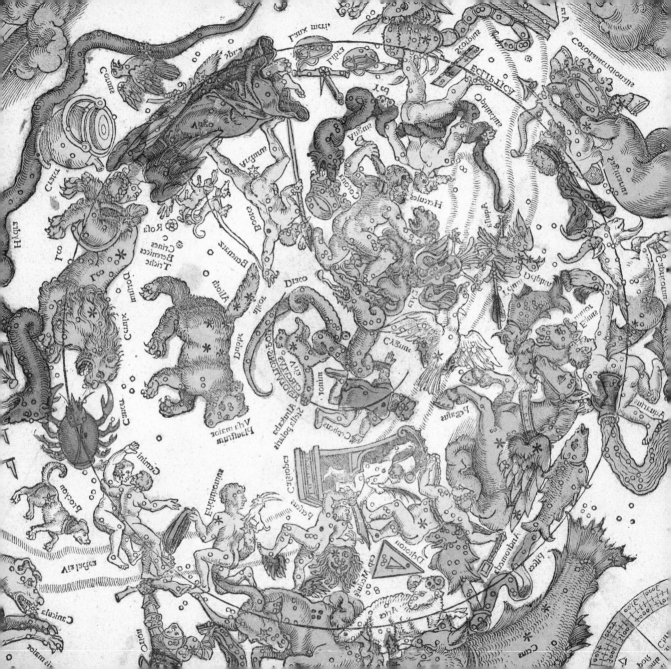

Peace on Earth

The Archer is wake!
The Swan is flying!
Gold against blue
An Arrow is lying.
There is hunting in heaven—
Sleep safe till tomorrow.

The Bears are abroad!
The Eagle is screaming!
Gold against blue
Their eyes are gleaming!
Sleep!
Sleep safe till tomorrow.

The Sisters lie
With their arms intertwining;
Gold against blue
Their hair is shining!
The Serpent writhes!
Orion is listening!
His sword is glistening!
Sleep!
There is hunting in heaven—
Sleep safe till tomorrow.

WILLIAM CARLOS WILLIAMS, American, 1883–1963

The Constellations and **Lunar Eclipse**
Details from hand-colored woodblock prints
Michael Ostendorfer, German, 1519–1559
From *Astronomicum Caesareum* (Imperial Astronomy)
by Petrus Apianus, German, 1501–1552
Ingolstadt, Bavaria, May 1540

The Duke on a Journey (detail)
From the *Belles Heures of Jean, duke of Berry*, fol. 223v
The Limbourg Brothers, France (Paris), active ca. 1400–1416
Tempera and gold on vellum

This Is the Key

This is the Key of the Kingdom:
In that Kingdom is a city;
In that city is a town;
In that town there is a street;
In that street there winds a lane;
In that lane there is a yard;
In that yard there is a house;
In that house there waits a room
In that room an empty bed
And on that bed a basket—
A Basket of Sweet Flowers;
 Of Flowers, of Flowers;
 A Basket of Sweet Flowers.

Flowers in a Basket;
Basket on the bed;
Bed in the chamber;
Chamber in the house;
House in the weedy yard;
Yard in the winding lane;
Lane in the broad street;
Street in the high town;
Town in the city;
City in the Kingdom—
This is the Key of the Kingdom;
 Of the Kingdom this is the Key.

ANONYMOUS, ENGLISH

A Basket of Flowers (detail)
Jan Brueghel the Younger, Flemish, 1601–1678
Oil on wood

Sunset on the Sea
John F. Kensett,
American, 1816–1872
Oil on canvas, 1872

On the Road

Though this land is not my own
I will never forget it,
or the waters of its ocean,
fresh and delicately icy.

Sand on the bottom is whiter
    than chalk,
and the air drunk, like wine.
Late sun lays bare
the rosy limbs of the pine trees.

And the sun goes down in waves
    of ether
in such a way that I can't tell
if the day is ending, or the world,
or if the secret of secrets is within
    me again.

ANNA AKHMATOVA, Russian, 1889–1966
    (Translated by Jane Kenyon)

Aristotle with a Bust of Homer (detail)
Rembrandt Harmensz. van Rijn, Dutch, 1606–1669
Oil on canvas, 1653

The Secrets of the World

Grand Is the Seen

Grand is the seen, the light, to me—grand are the sky and stars,
Grand is the earth, and grand are lasting time and space,
And grand their laws, so multiform, puzzling, evolutionary;
But grander far the unseen soul of me, comprehending, endowing all those,
Lighting the light, the sky and stars, delving the earth, sailing the sea,
(What were all those, indeed, without thee, unseen soul? of what amount without thee?)
More evolutionary, vast, puzzling, O my soul!
More multiform far—more lasting thou than they.

WALT WHITMAN, American, 1819–1892

Secretly We Spoke

Secretly we spoke,
    that wise one and me.
I said, *Tell me the secrets of the world.*
He said, *Sh . . . Let silence*
Tell you the secrets of the world.

JALAL-UD-DIN RUMI, Persian, 1207–1273
    (Translated by Jonathan Star and Shahram Shiva)

However Far You Go

However far you go, you will
never find the boundaries of the soul.

HERACLITUS, Greek, 6th–5th century B.C.

Kedar Regini: Page from a Dispersed Ragamala Series
Ruknuddin, Indian (Rajasthan, Bikaner), 1690–95
Ink and opaque watercolor on paper

Constellation: Toward the Rainbow
Joan Miró, Spanish, 1893–1983
Gouache and oil wash on paper, 1941

Poetry

And it was at that age . . .
    Poetry arrived
in search of me. I don't know,
    I don't know where
it came from, from winter
    or a river.
I don't know how or when,
no, they were not voices,
    they were not
words, nor silence,
but from a street I
    was summoned,
from the branches of night,
abruptly from the others,
among violent fires
or returning alone,
there I was without a face
and it touched me.

I did not know what to say,
    my mouth
had no way
with names,
my eyes were blind,
and something started in
    my soul,
fever or forgotten wings,
and I made my own way,
deciphering
that fire,
and I wrote the first
    faint line,

faint, without substance,
        pure nonsense,
pure wisdom

of someone who
        knows nothing,
and suddenly I saw
the heavens
unfastened
and open,
planets,
palpitating plantations,
shadow perforated,
riddled
with arrows, fire and flowers,
the winding night, the universe.

And I, infinitesimal being,
drunk with the great
        starry
                void,
likeness, image of
mystery,
felt myself a pure part
of the abyss,
I wheeled with the stars,
my heart broke loose on
        the wind.

PABLO NERUDA, Chilean, 1904–1973
        (Translated by Alistair Reid)

Portrait of a Young Man
Bronzino (Agnolo di Cosimo di Mariano),
Italian (Florentine), 1503–1572
Oil on wood

Vermeer

Quia respexit humilitatem ancillae suae. Luke 1:48

She stands by the table, poised
at the center of your vision,
with her left hand
just barely on
the pitcher's handle, and her right
lightly touching the windowframe.
Serene as a clear sky, luminous
in her blue dress and many-toned
white cotton wimple, she is looking
nowhere. Upon her lips
is the subtlest and most lovely
of smiles, caught
for an instant
like a snowflake in a warm hand.
How weightless her body feels
as she stands, absorbed, within this
fulfillment that has brought more
than any harbinger could.
She looks down with an infinite
tenderness in her eyes,
as though the light at the window
were a newborn child
and her arms open enough
to hold it on her breast forever.

STEPHEN MITCHELL, American, b. 1943

Young Woman with a Water Jug
Johannes Vermeer, Dutch, 1632–1675
Oil on canvas

I Love All Beauteous Things

I love all beauteous things,
    I seek and adore them;
God hath no better praise,
And man in his hasty days
    Is honoured for them.

I too will something make
    And joy in the making;
Altho' to-morrow it seem
Like the empty words of a dream
    Remembered on waking.

ROBERT BRIDGES, British, 1844–1930

Woman with a Lute
Johannes Vermeer, Dutch, 1632–1675
Oil on canvas

韓幹畫照夜白

The Master

When Han Kan was summoned
to the imperial capital
it was suggested he sit at the feet of
the illustrious senior court painter
to learn from him the refinements of the art.

"No, thank you," he replied,
"I shall apprentice myself to the stables."

And he installed himself and his brushes amid the dung and the flies,
and studied the horses—their bodies' keen alertness—
eye-sparkle of one, another's sensitive stance,
the way a third moved graceful in his bulk—

and painted at last the emperor's favorite,
the charger named "Nightshining White,"

whose likeness after centuries still dazzles.

FREDERICK MORGAN, American, b. 1922

Flower in the Crannied Wall

Flower in the crannied wall,
I pluck you out of the crannies,
I hold you here, root and all, in my hand,
Little flower—but if I could understand
What you are, root and all, and all in all,
I should know what God and man is.

ALFRED, LORD TENNYSON, English, 1809–1892

Something Like the Sun

The eye must be something like the sun,
Otherwise no sunlight could be seen;
God's own power must be inside us,
How else could Godly things delight us?

JOHANN WOLFGANG VON GOETHE, German, 1749–1832

Morning Glories
One of a pair of six-panel screens
Suzuki Kiitsu, Japanese, Edo period, 1796–1858,
Mineral pigment on gold-leafed paper

In a Thousand Forms

You may hide yourself in a thousand forms,
Still, All-beloved, I recognize you;
You may cover yourself in magic mists,
All-present, I can always tell that it is you.

I discover you as well, All-beautifully-growing,
In the cypress's pure young surge.
In the stream's fresh, living rush,
All-enchanting, I know you well.

When rising jets of water unfurl,
All-playful, how glad I am to see you;
When clouds form and transform themselves,
All-manifold, I discern you in them.

In the blossoming tapestry that covers the meadow,
I see your All-colorful, starry beauty;
When ivies reach their thousand arms around,
I meet you, All-embracing.

When morning lights the mountain range
I greet you there too, All-brightening,
Then, as the sky grows round above me,
All-heart-expanding, it is you I inhale.

What, with outer and inner senses, I know,
I know only through you, All-teaching;
When I name Allah's hundred names,
A name, with each name, re-echoes for you.

JOHANN WOLFGANG VON GOETHE, German, 1749–1832
    (Translated by John White)

The Four Trees
Claude Monet,
French, 1840–1926
Oil on canvas, 1891

Dogwoods
Window of leaded favrile glass
Tiffany Studios,
New York City, ca. 1900–15

Saint Francis Preaching to the Animals
Detail of a leaf from a Hungarian royal
manuscript with scenes of the life of Saint Francis
Italian, Bolognese School, ca. 1320–42
Tempera and gold leaf on parchment

Canticle of the Sun

Most high, all-powerful sweet Lord,
yours is the praise, the glory, and the honor
and every blessing.

Be praised, my Lord,
for all your creatures,
and first for brother sun,
who makes the day bright and luminous.

And he is beautiful and radiant
    with great splendor,
he is the image of you, Most High.

Be praised, my Lord,
for sister moon and the stars,
in the sky you have made them brilliant
    and precious and beautiful.

Be praised, my Lord, for brother wind
and for the air both cloudy and serene
    and every kind of weather,
through which you give nourishment
    to your creatures.

Be praised, my Lord, for sister water,
who is very useful and humble
    and precious and chaste.

Be praised, my Lord, for brother fire,
through whom you illuminate the night.
And he is beautiful and joyous
    and robust and strong.

Be praised, my Lord,
    for our sister, mother earth
who nourishes us and watches over us
and brings forth various fruits
    with colored flowers and herbs.

Be praised, my Lord,
    for those who forgive through
        your love,
and bear sickness and tribulation;

blessed are those who endure in peace,
for they will be crowned by you,
    Most High.

Be praised, my Lord,
    for our sister, bodily death,
from whom no living thing can escape.

Blessed are those whom she finds
    doing your most holy will,
for the second death cannot harm them.

Praise and bless my Lord
and give thanks to him and serve him
    with great humility.

FRANCIS OF ASSISI, Italian, 1182–1226
    (Translated by Stephen Mitchell)

The Grande Chartreuse (detail)
From the *Belles Heures of Jean, duke of Berry*, fol. 97v
The Limbourg Brothers, France (Paris), active ca. 1400–1416
Tempera and gold on vellum

Hear the Voice of the Bard!

Hear the voice of the Bard!
Who Present, Past, & Future sees,
Whose ears have heard
The Holy Word,
That walk'd among the ancient trees.

Calling the lapsed Soul
And weeping in the evening dew:
That might controll
The starry pole:
And fallen fallen light renew!

"O Earth O Earth return!
Arise from out the dewy grass;
Night is worn,
and the morn
Rises from the slumberous mass.

"Turn away no more:
Why wilt thou turn away?
The starry floor,
The watry shore,
Is giv'n thee till the break of day."

WILLIAM BLAKE, English, 1757–1827

The Voice of the Ancient Bard
William Blake, English, 1757–1827
Hand-colored relief etching,
heightened with gold,
from *Songs of Innocence
and of Experience,*
1789–94 (printed in 1825)

Zacharias and the Angel (detail)
William Blake, English, 1757–1827
Tempera and glue size on canvas

In a Dark Time

In a dark time, the eye begins to see,
I meet my shadow in the deepening shade;
I hear my echo in the echoing wood—
A lord of nature weeping to a tree.
I live between the heron and the wren,
Beasts of the hill and serpents of the den.

What's madness but nobility of soul
At odds with circumstance? The day's on fire!
I know the purity of pure despair,
My shadow pinned against a sweating wall.
That place among the rocks—is it a cave,
Or a winding path? The edge is what I have.

A steady stream of correspondences!
A night flowing with birds, a ragged moon,
And in broad day the midnight come again!
A man goes far to find out what he is—
Death of the self in a long, tearless night,
All natural shapes blazing unnatural light.

Dark, dark my light, and darker my desire.
My soul, like some heat-maddened summer fly,
Keeps buzzing at the sill. Which I is I?
A fallen man, I climb out of my fear.
The mind enters itself, and God the mind,
And one is One, freeing in the tearing wind.

THEODORE ROETHKE, American, 1908–1963

The Penitence of St. Jerome (detail)
Joachim Patinir, Netherlandish,
active by 1515, d. 1524
Oil on wood

Saint Anthony Abbot in the Wilderness
Osservanza Master, Italian (Sienese),
active second quarter of the 15th century
Tempera and gold on wood

Change

Do you think it is easy to change?
Ah, it is very hard to change and be different.
It means passing through the waters of oblivion.

D. H. LAWRENCE, English, 1885–1930

Island

Wave of sorrow,
Do not drown me now:

I see the island
Still ahead somehow.

I see the island
And its sands are fair:

Wave of sorrow,
Take me there.

LANGSTON HUGHES, American, 1902–1967

The Ferryman
Jean-Baptiste-Camille Corot,
French, 1796–1875
Oil on canvas

The Great Wave off Kanagawa (detail)
Katsushika Hokusai,
Japanese, 1760–1849
Colored woodblock print from
Thirty-six Views of Fuji,
1823–29, Edo period

Wisdom Speaks

The Lord possessed me in the beginning of his way,
Before his works of old.
I was set up from everlasting,
From the beginning,
Or ever the earth was.
When there were no depths, I was brought forth;
When there were no fountains abounding with water.
Before the mountains were settled,
Before the hills was I brought forth:
While as yet he had not made the earth, nor the fields,
Nor the highest part of the dust of the world.
When he prepared the heavens, I was there:
When he set a compass upon the face of the depth:
When he established the clouds above:
When he strengthened the fountains of the deep:
When he gave to the sea his decree,
That the waters should not pass his commandment:
When he appointed the foundations of the earth:
Then I was by him,
As one brought up with him:
And I was daily his delight,
Rejoicing always before him;
Rejoicing in the habitable part of his earth;
And my delights were with the sons of men.

PROVERBS 8: 22-31

Oleanders; L'Arlésienne: Madame Joseph-Michel Ginoux
(Marie Julien, 1848–1911)
Vincent van Gogh, Dutch, 1853–1890
Oil on canvas

When I Have Fears
That I May Cease to Be

When I have fears that I may cease to be
    Before my pen has gleaned my teeming brain,
Before high-piled books, in charactery,
    Hold like rich garners the full ripened grain;
When I behold, upon the night's starred face,
    Huge cloudy symbols of a high romance,
And think that I may never live to trace
    Their shadows, with the magic hand of chance;
And when I feel, fair creature of an hour,
    That I shall never look upon thee more,
Never have relish in the faery power
    Of unreflecting love;—then on the shore
Of the wide world I stand alone, and think
Till love and fame to nothingness do sink.

JOHN KEATS, English, 1795–1821

Sometimes

Sometimes I go about pitying myself,
and all the time
I am being carried on great winds across the sky.

ANONYMOUS, CHIPPEWA INDIAN
    (Adapted by Robert Bly from Frances Densmore's translation)

Landscape—Scene from "Thanatopsis"
Asher Brown Durand, American, 1796–1886
Oil on canvas, 1850

Spider and Grapevine
Taki Katei, Japanese, 1830–1901
Leaf from *Album of Flower and Bird Paintings*
Ink and color on silk

A Noiseless Patient Spider

A noiseless patient spider,
I mark'd where on a little promontory it stood isolated,
Mark'd how to explore the vacant vast surrounding,
It launch'd forth filament, filament, filament, out of itself,
Ever unreeling them, ever tirelessly speeding them.

And you O my soul where you stand,
Surrounded, detached, in measureless oceans of space,
Ceaselessly musing, venturing, throwing, seeking the spheres to connect them,
Till the bridge you will need be form'd, till the ductile anchor hold,
Till the gossamer thread you fling catch somewhere, O my soul.

WALT WHITMAN, American, 1819–1892

In Age I Bud Again

FROM THE FLOWER

Who would have thought my shrivelled heart
Could have recovered greenness? It was gone
    Quite under ground, as flowers depart
To feed their mother-root when they have blown,
        Where they together
        All the hard weather
Dead to the world, keep house unknown.

These are thy wonders, Lord of Power,
Killing and quickening, bringing down to hell
    And up to heaven in an hour;
Making a chiming of a passing-bell.
        We say amiss,
        This or that is:
Thy word is all, if we could spell.
        ....
And now in age I bud again,
After so many deaths I live and write;
    I once more smell the dew and rain,
And relish versing: O my only Light,
        It cannot be
        That I am he
On whom thy tempests fell all night.

GEORGE HERBERT, English, 1593–1633

Parrots and Magnolias
Detail from a leaded-glass window
Tiffany Studios, New York City, ca. 1910–20

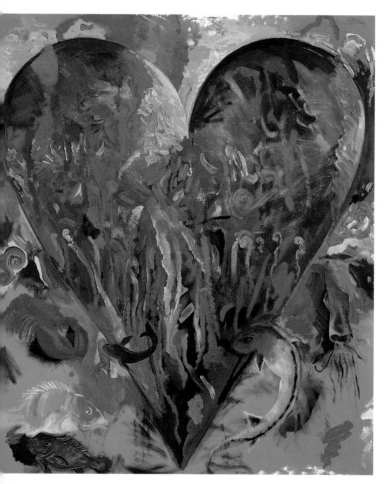

The Heart, South of Naples
Jim Dine, American, b. 1935
Oil on canvas, 1986

Explosion

If life is love, long live love!
I want more life to love! Today I see
that a thousand years of thinking
matter less than one blue instant of feeling.

My heart was slowly, sadly dying . . .
Today it opens like a flower of sunshine.
Life bursts open like a turbulent ocean
that the hand of love has thrust into motion!

Today my sadness, its wings broken,
fled into the cold gloom of night;
now the last trace of sorrow

fades away into faraway darkness . . .
My whole life is singing, kissing, laughing!
My whole life is a mouth in blossom!

DELMIRA AGUSTINI, Uruguayan, 1886–1914

The Garden of Love (Improvisation Number 27)
Wassily Kandinsky, Russian, 1866–1944
Oil on canvas, 1912

Gone, Gone, Gone

"Search for the longing, O you who love me." Old Saint

When the wind-sleeve moves in the
    morning street,
I walk there, and brood on brown things,
On green things,
On the green waves
Lifting at sea, the green wives, and the
    brood of heaven.

I hear a faint sound, a bell inside the waves
Coming from far off . . .and the sweet clear
Bell of the joys
Of silence pierces
Through the roaring of cars, the hum of tires,
    the closing of doors.

When I hear that sound, a subtle force, a sheath,
Motherly, wraps me. Inside that sheath
I need no
House or land,
Caught in sweetness as the trout in the
    running stream.

ROBERT BLY, American, b. 1926

Mystery of the Street
Umbo (Otto Umbehr), German, 1902–1980
Gelatin silver print

West Point (Casco Bay), Maine
John Marin, American, 1870–1953
Watercolor on paper, 1914

The Star

I had fallen asleep one night near the sea.
A cool wind woke me; leaving my dream,
I opened my eyes and saw the morning star
Glittering in the far depths of the sky
In a soft whiteness, infinite and lovely.
The north wind fled, taking the storm with it.
The blazing star turned stormclouds to down.
It was a light which thought and lived;
It calmed the waves breaking on the reef;
It was like seeing a soul through a pearl.
It was night, but darkness could not rule,
For the sky lit up with a divine smile.
The glow turned the tilting mast silver;
The ship was dark but the sail was white;
Attentive seagulls perching on a cliff
Gazed solemnly at the star, as if
It were a heavenly bird made of sparks.
Like a crowd of admirers, the ocean came closer
And, roaring softly, watched it shine,
As if afraid of scaring it away.

An indescribable love was everywhere;
Green grass shivered in bliss at my feet.
Birds talked in their nests; a flower
Woke up to tell me: it is my sister, the star.
And as darkness lifted its long folded veil,
I heard a voice come from the star
Saying: I am the star that comes first.
I am the one believed in the tomb, now empty.
I shone on Sinai, I shone on Taygeta;
I am the fiery gold pebble that God hurled
From a catapult into night's black facade.
I am what is reborn when a world is destroyed.

Oh, Nations! I am the Poetry of Devotion.
I shone on Moses and I shone on Dante.
The lion-like ocean is in love with me.
I come. Rise, Virtue, Courage, Faith!
Thinkers, Spirits — Climb the ramparts!
Eyelids, open! Eyes, alight! Earth,
Plow your furrows; start the fanfare, Life!
Sleepers, arise! — For the one who follows,
The one who sends me ahead,
Is the angel of Freedom, the giant of Light.

VICTOR HUGO, French, 1802–1885

Waves
Detail of a two-fold screen
Ogata Kōrin, Japanese, Edo period, 1658–1716
Ink, color, and gold leaf on paper

Star
Detail from a basin
Iranian, early 14th century
Brass, inlaid with silver and gold

The Titan's Goblet
Thomas Cole, American, 1801–1848
Oil on canvas, 1833

Now It Is Time That Gods Came Walking

Now it is time that gods came walking out
of lived-in Things . . .
Time that they came and knocked down every wall
inside my house. New page. Only the wind
from such a turning could be strong enough
to toss the air as a shovel tosses dirt:
a fresh-turned field of breath. O gods, gods!
who used to come so often and are still
asleep in the Things around us, who serenely
rise and at wells that we can only guess at
splash icy water on your necks and faces,
and lightly add your restedness to what seems
already filled to bursting: our full lives.
Once again let it be your morning, gods.
We keep repeating. You alone are source.
With you the world arises, and your dawn
gleams on each crack and crevice of our failure . . .

Rainer Maria Rilke, Austrian, 1875–1926
(Translated by Stephen Mitchell)

The Lake of Zug (detail)
Joseph Mallord William Turner,
English, 1775–1851
Watercolor, gouache, and colored chalk, 1843

A Further Sea

As If the Sea Should Part

As if the Sea should part
And show a further Sea—
And that — a further — and the Three
But a presumption be —

Of Periods of Seas —
Unvisited of Shores —
Themselves the Verge of Seas to be —
Eternity — is Those —

EMILY DICKINSON, American, 1830–1886

Unicorns (Legend—Sea Calm)
Arthur B. Davies, American, 1862–1928
Oil on canvas, ca. 1906

The Secret Land

Every woman of true royalty owns
A secret land more real to her
Than this pale outer world:

At midnight when the house falls quiet
She lays aside needle or book
And visits it unseen.

Shutting her eyes, she improvises
A five-barred gate among tall birches,
Vaults over, takes possession.

Then runs, or flies, or mounts a horse
(A horse will canter up to greet her)
And travels where she will;

Can make grass grow, coax lilies up
From bud to blossom as she watches,
Lets fish eat from her palm.

Madame Arthur Fontaine (Marie Escudier)
Odilon Redon, French, 1840–1916
Pastel on paper, 1901

108

Has founded villages, planted groves
And hollowed valleys for brooks running
Cool to a land-locked bay.

I never dared question my love
About the government of her queendom
Or its geography,

Nor followed her between those birches,
Setting one leg astride the gate,
Spying into the mist.

Yet she has pledged me, when I die,
A lodge beneath her private palace
In a level clearing of the wood
Where gentians grow and gillyflowers
And sometimes we may meet.

ROBERT GRAVES, British, 1895–1986

A Hawking Party
Detail from a tapestry
South Netherlandish, 1500–1530
Wool warp, wool wefts

Amaryllis
Mary Frank, American, b. 1933
Color monotype on two sheets, 1977

Bulbs

I have planted lilies, but will they all grow well with me?
Will they like the glitter of this north-looking hillside?
Will they like the rude winds, the stir, the quick changes?
Would they not have shadowy stillnesses, and peace?

      Lilium chalcedonicum, calla aethiopica,
      Lilium auratum, candidum, the martagon,
      Lilium speciosum, pardalinum, umbellatum,
      Amaryllis, convalleria, nerine.

All these lovely lilies. I wish that they would grow with me,
No other flowers have the texture of the lilies,
The heart-piercing fragrance, the newly alighted angel's
Lineal poise, and purity, and peace—

      (We wait their pleasure. Yet if they grow not
      Need only take patience a little while longer;
      For these are the flowers we look to find blooming
      In the meadows and lanes that lie beyond Jordan—
      All kinds of lilies in the lanes that lead gently,
      Very gently, by degrees, in the shade of green trees,
      To the foothills and fields of Paradise.)

MARY URSULA BETHELL, New Zealand, 1874–1945

Paradise (detail)
Giovanni di Paolo (Giovanni di Paolo di Grazia),
Italian (Sienese), active by 1417, d. 1482
Tempera and gold on canvas, transferred from wood

In the Beginning

FROM WORKS AND DAYS

In the beginning, the immortals
    who have their homes on Olympus
created the golden generation of
    mortal people.
These lived in Kronos' time, when he
    was the king in heaven.
They lived as if they were gods,
    their hearts free from all sorrow,
by themselves, and without hard work
    or pain; no miserable
old age came their way; their hands,
    their feet, did not alter.
They took their pleasure in festivals,
    and lived without troubles.
When they died, it was as if they
    fell asleep. All goods
were theirs. The fruitful grainland
    yielded its harvest to them
of its own accord; this was great
    and abundant, while they at
        their pleasure
quietly looked after their works
    in the midst of good things,
prosperous in flocks, on friendly terms
    with the blessed immortals.

Now that the earth has gathered
    over this generation,
these are called pure and blessed spirits;
    they live upon earth,
and are good, they watch over mortal men
    and defend them from evil.

HESIOD, Greek, eighth century B.C.
    (Translated by Richard Lattimore)

Fragments of a Skyphos
Attributed to the Palermo Painter
Greek (South Italian), last third of the fifth century B.C.
Terracotta

To Aphrodite

Leave Crete,
Aphrodite,
and come to this
sacred place
encircled by apple trees,
fragrant with offered smoke.

Here, cold springs
sing softly
amid the branches;
the ground is shady with roses;
from trembling young leaves,
a deep drowsiness pours.

In the meadow,
horses are cropping
the wildflowers of spring,
scented fennel
blows on the breeze.

In this place,
Lady of Cyprus, pour
the nectar that honors you
into our cups,
gold, and raised up for drinking.

SAPPHO, Greek, 7th century B.C.
(Translated by Jane Hirshfield)

Landscape Vignette
Detail of a fresco from the
Imperial Villa at Boscotrecase, Roman,
last decade of the first century B.C.

How Like an Angel Came I Down!
From Wonder

How like an angel came I down!
　How bright are all things here!
When first among His works I did appear,
　Oh, how their glory me did crown!
The world resembled His eternity,
　In which my soul did walk;
And everything that I did see
　　Did with me talk.

The skies in their magnificence,
　The lively, lovely air,
Oh, how divine, how soft, how sweet,
　　how fair!
　The stars did entertain my sense,
And all the works of God, so bright and pure,
　So rich and great did seem,
As if they must endure
　　In my esteem.

A native health and innocence
　Within my bones did grow;
And while my God did all His glories show,
　I felt a vigor in my sense
That was all spirit. I within did flow
　With seas of life, like wine;
I nothing in the world did know
　　But 'twas divine.

Harsh ragged objects were concealed,
　　Oppression's tears and cries,
Sins, griefs, complaints, dissensions, weeping eyes
　　Were hid, and only things revealed
Which heavenly spirits and the angels prize.
　　　The state of innocence
And bliss, not trades and poverties,
　　　Did fill my sense.

The streets were paved with golden stones;
　　The boys and girls were mine,
Oh, how did all their lovely faces shine!
　　The sons of men were holy ones,
In joy and beauty they appeared to me,
　　　And everything which here I found,
　　While like an angel I did see,
　　　Adorned the ground.

　　　　　..............

Proprieties themselves were mine,
　　And hedges, ornaments;
Walls, boxes, coffers, and their rich contents
　　Did not divide my joys, but all combine.
Clothes, ribbons, jewels, laces, I esteemed
　　My joys by others worn:
For me they all to wear them seemed
　　When I was born.

THOMAS TRAHERNE, English, 1637–1674

Woman and Child with a Stroller
and **Little Girls at a Fountain**
Maurice Prendergast, American, 1859–1924
Watercolor on paper from the *Large Boston
Public Garden Sketchbook*, 1895–97

Autumn

The leaves are falling, falling as if from far up,
as if orchards were dying high in space.
Each leaf falls as if it were motioning "no."

And tonight the heavy earth is falling
away from all the other stars in the loneliness.

We're all falling. This hand here is falling.
And look at the other one . . . It's in them all.

And yet there is Someone, whose hands
infinitely calm, hold up all this falling.

RAINER MARIA RILKE, Austrian, 1875–1926
    (Translated by Robert Bly)

To the Heavens

Clear fountain of beautiful new light,
Heavenly land, full of shining!
House of truth, without shadow or veil,
Where wise spirits happily reside!

Oh, how far you are, glorious land,
how far from useless mortal striving,
like a divine Argus, rising and flying,
holy, and free from all human failings.

Oh beloved home! Longing for you only,
this pilgrim soul is locked in its prison,
further astray, from minute to minute.

May the perfect beauty that I love so dearly
someday grant me the possibility of being
the lover who climbs to the height of the beloved.

FRANCISCO DE ALDANA, Spanish, 1537–1578

Indian Summer
William Trost Richards, American, 1833–1905
Oil on canvas, 1875

Allegory of the Planets and Continents (detail)
Giovanni Battista Tiepolo, Italian (Venetian), 1696–1770
Oil on canvas

Nocturn

Night comes, an angel stands
Measuring out the time of stars,
Still are the winds, and still the hours.

It would be peace to lie
Still in the still hours at the angel's feet,
Upon a star hung in a starry sky,
But hearts another measure beat.

Each body, wingless as it lies,
Sends out its butterfly of night
With delicate wings and jewelled eyes.

And some upon day's shores are cast,
And some in darkness lost
In waves beyond the world, where float
Somewhere the islands of the blest.

KATHLEEN RAINE, English, b. 1908

Poem

Let nothing disturb thee,
Nothing affright thee;
All things are passing;
God never changeth;
Patient endurance
Attaineth to all things;
Who God possesseth
In nothing is wanting;
Alone God sufficeth.

TERESA OF ÁVILA, Spanish, 1515–1582
(Translated by Henry Wadsworth Longfellow)

Angel
Detail from the central panel of *The Pérussis Altarpiece*
French, 1480
Oil and gold on wood

The Magic Flute (detail)
Set design for the entrance of the Queen of the Night
Karl Friedrich Thiele, active 1780–1836, Berlin
after Karl Friedrich Schinkel, German, 1781–1841
Hand- and plate-colored aquatint, 1819

The Paradise Within: Adam Speaks with the Angel

FROM PARADISE LOST

Study of an Angel
Annibale Carracci, Italian (Bolognese), 1560–1609
Black chalk, heightened with white, on blue paper

"Greatly instructed I shall hence depart,
Greatly in peace of thought, and have my fill
Of knowledge, what this vessel can contain;
Beyond which was my folly to aspire.
Henceforth I learn that to obey is best,
And love with fear the only God, to walk
As in his presence, ever to observe
His providence, and on him sole depend,
Merciful over all his works, with good
Still overcoming evil, and by small
Accomplishing great things—by things deemed weak
Subverting worldly-strong, and worldly-wise
By simply meek; that suffering for Truth's sake
Is fortitude to highest victory,
And to the faithful death the gate of life—
Taught this by his example whom I now
Acknowledge my Redeemer ever blest."
To whom thus also th' Angel last replied:—
"This having learned, thou has attained the sum
Of wisdom; hope no higher, though all the stars
Thou Knew'st by name, and all th' ethereal powers,
All secrets of the deep, all Nature's works,
Or works of God in heaven, air, earth, or sea,
And all the riches of this world enjoy'dst,
And all the rule, one empire. Only add
Deeds to thy knowledge answerable; add faith;
Add virtue, patience, temperance; add love,
By name to come called Charity, the soul
Of all the rest: then wilt thou not be loth
To leave this Paradise, but shalt possess
A Paradise within thee, happier far."

JOHN MILTON, English, 1608–1674

The Creation and the Expulsion of Adam and Eve from Paradise (detail)
Giovanni di Paolo (Giovanni di Paolo di Grazia),
Italian (Sienese), active by 1417, d. 1482
Tempera and gold on wood

Saint John on Patmos (detail)
From *The Cloisters Apocalypse*, fol. 3r
France, Normandy (Manche),
Coutances, 1300–1325
Tempera, gold, silver, and ink on vellum

And I Saw a New Heaven and a New Earth

FROM THE REVELATION OF SAINT JOHN THE DIVINE

And I saw a new heaven and a new earth
For the first heaven and the first earth were
    passed away;
And there was no more sea.

And I John saw the holy city,
New Jerusalem
Coming down from God out of heaven,
Prepared as a bride adorned for her husband.

And I heard a great voice out of heaven saying,
Behold, the tabernacle of God is with men,
And he will dwell with them,
And they shall be his people,
And God himself shall be with them,
And be their God.

And God shall wipe away all tears from
    their eyes;
And there shall be no more death,
Neither sorrow, nor crying,
Neither shall there be any more pain:
For the former things are passed away.

And he that sat upon the throne said,
Behold, I make all things new.
And he said unto me,
Write: for these words are true and faithful.

And he said unto me,
It is done.
I am Alpha and Omega,
The beginning and the end.
I will give unto him that is athirst
Of the fountain of the water of life freely.

REVELATION 21: 1-6

Saint John on Patmos
Hans Baldung (called Grien),
German, 1484/85–1545
Oil on wood

Landscape
Detail from a favrile glass mosaic
Tiffany Studios, New York City, 1905–15

Tell Me, O Swan

Tell me, O Swan, your ancient tale.
From what land do you come, O Swan?
    to what shore will you fly?
Where would you take your rest, O
    Swan, and what do you seek?

Even this morning, O Swan, awake,
    arise, follow me!
There is a land where no doubt nor
    sorrow have rule: where the terror
        of Death is no more.

There the woods of spring are a-bloom,
    and the fragrant scent "He is I"
        is borne on the wind:
There the bee of the heart is deeply
    immersed, and desires no other joy.

KABIR, Persian, ca. 1400
    (Translated by Rabindranath Tagore)

The Last Invocation

At the last, tenderly,
From the walls of the powerful
    fortress'd house,
From the clasp of the knitted locks,
    from the keep
    of the well-closed doors,
Let me be wafted.

Let me glide noiselessly forth;
With the key of softness unlock
    the locks—with a whisper,
Set ope the doors O soul.

Tenderly—be not impatient,
(Strong is your hold O mortal flesh.
Strong is your hold O love.)

WALT WHITMAN, American, 1819–1892

**Bahrām Gūr Visits the Persian
Princess in the Purple Palace**
Leaf from a *Khamsa* (Five Poems)
of Amīr Khusrau of Delhi
Indian, Mughal, period of Akbar, 1597–98
Ink, colors, and gold on paper

Written to the Tune "The Fisherman's Honor"

The sky becomes one with its clouds,
the waves with their mist.
In Heaven's starry river, a thousand sails dance.
As if dreaming, I return to the place
where the Highest lives,
and hear a voice from the heavens:
Where am I going?
I answer, "The road is long,"
and sigh; soon the sun will be setting.
Hard to find words in poems to carry amazement:
on its ninety-thousand-mile wind,
the huge inner bird is soaring.
O wind, do not stop—
My little boat of raspberry wood
has not yet reached the Immortal Islands.

LI QINGZHAO, Chinese, 1084–1115?
    (Translated by Jane Hirshfield)

The Great Sea

The great sea has set me in motion,
set me adrift,
moving me like a weed in a river.

The sky and the strong wind
have moved the spirit inside me
till I am carried away
trembling with joy.

UVAVNUK, Eskimo, 19th–early 20th century
    (Translated by Stephen Mitchell)

Riverbank of Peach Blossoms
Leaf from the album *Wilderness Colors*
Shih-t'ao (Tao-chi), Chinese, 1642–1707
Ink and colors on paper

Peach Blossom Spring
Detail of a leaf from the album *Landscapes*
Fan Ch'i, Chinese, 1616–after 1694
Ink and colors on paper, 1646

127

The Penitence of St. Jerome (detail)
Joachim Patinir, Netherlandish,
active by 1515, d. 1524
Oil on wood

Heaven

O who will show me those delights on high?
    Echo.   I.
Thou Echo, thou art mortal, all men know.
    Echo.   No.
Wert thou not born among the trees and leaves?
    Echo.   Leaves.
And are there any leaves, that still abide?
    Echo.   Bide.
What leaves are they? impart the matter wholly.
    Echo.   Holy.
Are holy leaves the Echo then of bliss?
    Echo.   Yes.
Then tell me, what is that supreme delight?
    Echo.   Light.
Light to the mind: what shall the will enjoy?
    Echo.   Joy.
But are there cares and business with the pleasure?
    Echo.   Leisure.
Light, joy, and leisure; but shall they persevere?
    Echo.   Ever.

GEORGE HERBERT, English, 1593–1633

The Love of God

FROM PARADISO

The love of God, unutterable and perfect,
   flows into a pure soul the way that light
   rushes into a transparent object.
The more love that it finds, the more it gives
   itself; so that, as we grow clear and open,
   the more complete the joy of loving is.
And the more souls who resonate together,
   the greater the intensity of their love,
   for, mirror-like, each soul reflects the others.

DANTE ALIGHIERI, Italian, 1265–1321

   (Translated by Stephen Mitchell)

Dante and Beatrice with the Blessed Souls
Woodcut from Dante Alighieri, *Comedia dell'Inferno,
del Purgatorio, & del Paradiso* (Canto 27 of *Paradiso*)
Venice: Giovambattista, Marchio Sessa, & Fratelli, 1578

Angels
Details from *Madonna and Child with Angels*
Pietro di Domenico da Montepulciano, Italian (Marchigian),
active first quarter 15th century
Tempera on wood, gold ground

Songs Eternity

What is songs eternity
Come and see
Can it noise and bustle be
Come and see
Praises sung or praises said
Can it be
Wait awhile and these are dead
Sigh Sigh
Be they high or lowly bred
They die

What is songs eternity
Come and see
Melodys of earth and sky
Here they be
Songs once sung to adams ears
Can it be
—Ballads of six thousand years
Thrive thrive
Songs awakened with the spheres
Alive

Mighty songs that miss decay
What are they
Crowds and citys pass away
Like a day
Books are writ and books are read
What are they
Years will lay them with the dead
Sigh sigh
Trifles unto nothing wed
They die

Dreamers list the honey be
Mark the tree
Where the blue cap tootle tee
Sings a glee
Sung to adam and to eve
Here they be
When floods covered every bough
Noahs ark
Heard that ballad singing now
Hark hark

Tootle tootle tootle tee
Can it be
Pride and fame must shadows be
Come and see
Every season own her own
Bird and be

Sing creations music on
Natures glee
Is in every mood and tone
Eternity

The eternity of song
Liveth here
Natures universal tongue
Singeth here
Songs Ive heard and felt and seen
Everywhere
Songs like the grass are evergreen
The giver
Said live and be and they have been
For ever

JOHN CLARE, English, 1793–1864

The Wheel

At the first strokes of the fiddle bow
the dancers rise from their seats.
The dance begins to shape itself
in the crowd, as couples join,
and couples join couples, their movement
together lightening their feet.
They move in the ancient circle
of the dance. The dance and the song
call each other into being. Soon
they are one—rapt in a single
rapture, so that even the night
has its clarity, and time
is the wheel that brings it round.
In this rapture the dead return.
Sorrow is gone from them.
They are light. They step
into the steps of the living
and turn with them in the dance
in the sweet enclosure
of the song, and timeless
is the wheel that brings it round.

WENDELL BERRY, American, b. 1934

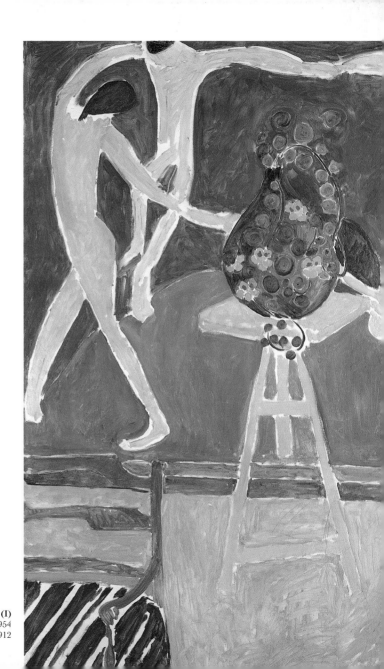

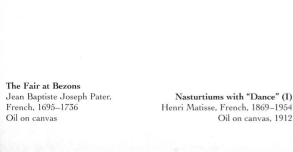

The Fair at Bezons
Jean Baptiste Joseph Pater,
French, 1695–1736
Oil on canvas

Nasturtiums with "Dance" (I)
Henri Matisse, French, 1869–1954
Oil on canvas, 1912

Bahrām Gūr with the Indian Princess in Her Black Pavilion
Leaf from a *Khamsa* (Five Poems) of Niẓamī
Persian, Timurid period, ca. 1440
Ink, colors, and gold on paper

Angels
Detail from *The Night Journey of Muḥammad on His Steed Burāq*,
leaf from the Būstan of Sāʿdī, copied by the calligrapher
Sultān-Muḥammad Nūr; probably painted in Central Asia
(Bukhara), 1520–40
Ink, colors, and gold on paper

You and I

Happy is the moment, when we sit together,
With two forms, two faces, yet one soul,
    you and I.

The flowers will bloom forever,
The birds will sing their eternal song,
The moment we enter the garden,
    you and I.

The stars of heaven will come to watch us,
And we will show them
    the light of a full moon—
    you and I.

No more thought of "you" and "I."
Just the bliss of union—
Joyous, alive, free of care, you and I.

All the bright-winged birds of heaven
Will swoop down to drink of our sweet water—
The tears of our laughter, you and I.

What a miracle of fate, us sitting here.
Even at the opposite ends of the earth
We would still be together, you and I.

We have one form in this world,
    another in the next.
To us belong an eternal heaven,
    the endless delight of you and I.

JALAL-UD-DIN RUMI, Persian, 1207–1273
    (Translated by Jonathan Star and Shahram Shiva)

Bamboo Yards, Kyōbashi Bridge
Utagawa Hiroshige, Japanese, 1797–1858
Woodblock print in colors from the series
One Hundred Famous Views of Edo, 1857

If Someone Asks

If someone asks
My abode
I reply:
"The east edge of
The Milky Way."

Like a drifting cloud,
Bound by nothing:
I just let go
Giving myself up
To the whim of the wind.

RYOKAN, Japanese, 1758–1831
    (Translated by John Stevens)

Moon Night

It was as if the sky
Had quietly kissed the earth,
So that she in her shimmer of blossoms
Would dream of nothing but him.

Breezes blew over the field,
Gently the corn ears swayed,
Soft rustles ran through the forest,
So starry and clear was the night.

And my soul spread
Its wings out wide
And flew through the peaceful country,
As though it were flying home.

JOSEPH VON EICHENDORFF, German, 1788–1857
(Translated by John White)

Landscape with Mount Fuji
Japanese, early 19th century
Exterior of a writing box cover;
sprinkled gold on lacquer

ACKNOWLEDGMENTS

Grateful acknowledgment is made to the following for permission to print the copyrighted material listed below. Every effort has been made to contact the original copyright holders of the materials included.

Mary Ursula Bethell: "Bulbs" reprinted by permission of the Trustees in the estate of the late Mary Ursula Bethell.

Robert Bly: "Sometimes." Reprinted from *The Sea and the Honeycomb: A Book of Tiny Poems*, edited by Robert Bly, Beacon Press, 1971. Version copyright 1971 by Robert Bly, adapted from the Frances Densmore translation. Reprinted with Robert Bly's permission.

Bureau of American Ethnology: "The Child Is Introduced to the Cosmos at Birth" reprinted from the *27th Annual Report of the Bureau of Ethnology*, 1911.

Jonathan Cape: "Adagio" from *Herman Hesse: Poems Selected and Translated by James Wright*. Reprinted by permission of Jonathan Cape, an imprint of Random House UK Ltd. "Poetry" from Selected Poems by Pablo Neruda, translated by Alistair Reid. Reprinted by permission of Jonathan Cape, an imprint of Random House UK Ltd.

Carcanet Press Limited: "Peace on Earth" by William Carlos Williams from *The Collected Poems of William Carlos Williams*, 1986. Reprinted by permission of Carcanet Press Limited, Manchester. "The Secret Land" by Robert Graves. Copyright © The Estate of Robert Graves. Reprinted by permission of Carcanet Press Limited, Manchester.

City Lights Books: "When, With You Asleep" by Juan Ramón Jiménez. English translation Copyright © 1986 by Perry Higman. Reprinted by permission of City Lights Books.

Copper Canyon Press: "Sometimes" from *Selected Poems 1938–1988* © 1988 by Thomas McGrath.

Reprinted by permission of Copper Canyon Press, PO Box 271, Port Townsend, WA 98368.

Doubleday: "In a Dark Time," copyright © 1960 by Beatrice Roethke, Admistratrix of the Estate of Theodore Roethke, from *The Collected Poems of Theodore Roethke* by Theodore Roethke. Used by permission of Doubleday, a division of Bantam Doubleday Dell Publishing Group, Inc. "The Waking," copyright 1948 by Theodore Roethke, from *The Collected Poems of Theodore Roethke* by Theodore Roethke. Used by permission of Doubleday, a division of Bantam Doubleday Dell Publishing Group, Inc.

The Ecco Press: "On Angels" from *The Collected Poems* by Czeslaw Milosz. Copyright © 1988 by Czeslaw Milosz Royalties, Inc. First published by The Ecco Press in 1988. Reprinted by permission.

Faber and Faber Limited: "The Brave Man" by Wallace Stevens. Reprinted by permission of Faber and Faber Ltd. from *The Collected Poems of Wallace Stevens*. "In a Dark Time" and "The Waking" by Theodore Roethke. Reprinted by permission of Faber and Faber Ltd. from *The Collected Poems of Theodore Roethke*.

Farrar, Straus & Giroux, Inc.: "The Wheel" from *The Collected Poems, 1957–1982* by Wendell Berry. Copyright © 1984 by Wendell Berry. Reprinted by permission of North Point Press, a division of Farrar, Straus & Giroux, Inc. "Adagio," an excerpt from "Holiday Music in the Evening" from *Poems* by Herman Hesse, translated by James Wright. Translation copyright © 1970 by James Wright. Reprinted by permission of Farrar, Straus & Giroux, Inc. "The Angels" from *The Book of Images* by Rainer Maria Rilke, translated by Edward Snow. Translation copyright © 1991 by Edward Snow. Reprinted by permission of North Point Press, a division of Farrar, Straus & Giroux, Inc.

Donald Hall: "On the Road" by Anna Akhmatova, translated by Jane Kenyon. Translation copyright © 1985. Reprinted by permission of Donald Hall.

CREDITS

Page 72   Purchase, Lila Acheson Wallace Gift, 1972   1972.125

Page 73   Gift of Mr. and Mrs. Peter Findlay, 1978   1978.540.2

Page 74   The Jacques and Natasha Gelman Collection

Page 75   H. O. Havemeyer Collection, Bequest of
Mrs. H. O. Havemeyer, 1929   29.100.16

Page 76   Marquand Collection, Gift of Henry G. Marquand,
1889   89.15.21

Page 77   Bequest of Collis P. Huntington, 1900   25.110.24

Page 78   Purchase, The Dillon Fund Gift, 1977   1977.78

Page 79   Purchase, The Dillon Fund Gift, 1989   1989.141.3

Page 80-81   Seymour Fund, 1954   54.69.2

Page 82   H. O. Havemeyer Collection, Bequest of
Mrs. H. O. Havemeyer, 1929   29.100.110

Page 83   Gift of Frank Stanton, in memory of
Ruth Stephenson Stanton, 1995   1995.204

Page 84   The Cloisters Collection, 1954   54.1.1

Page 85   Gift of Mr. and Mrs. Edwin L. Weisl Jr., 1994   1994.516

Page 86   Bequest of William Church Osborn, 1951   51.30.1

Page 87   Rogers Fund, 1917   17.10.54

Page 88   Fletcher Fund, 1936   36.14a–c

Page 89   Robert Lehman Collection, 1975   1975.1.27

Page 90   H. O. Havemeyer Collection, Bequest of
Mrs. H. O. Havemeyer, 1929   JP1847

Page 91   Bequest of Benjamin Altman, 1913   14.40.811

Page 92   Gift of Mr. and Mrs. John L. Loeb, 1962   62.24

Page 93   Bequest of Sam A. Lewisohn, 1951   51.112.3

Page 94–95   Gift of J. Pierpont Morgan, 1911   11.156

Page 96   Gift of Dr. and Mrs. Harold B. Bilsky, 1975   1975.282.1h

Page 97   Gift of Earl and Lucille Sydnor, 1990   1990.315

Page 98   Anonymous Gift, 1986   1986.404

Page 99   Alfred Stieglitz Collection, 1949   49.70.1

Page 100   Bequest of Charles F. Iklé, 1963   64.27.3

Page 101   Ford Motor Company Collection, Gift of Ford
Motor Company and John C. Waddell, 1987   1987.1100.49

Page 102   Fletcher Fund, 1926   26.117

Page 103   Edward C. Moore Collection, Bequest of
Edward C. Moore, 1891   91.1.521

Page 104   Gift of Samuel P. Avery Jr., 1904   04.29.2

Page 105   Marquand Fund, 1959   59.120

Page 106–107   Bequest of Lillie P. Bliss, 1931   31.67.12

Page 108   The Mr. and Mrs. Henry Ittleson Jr. Purchase Fund,
1960   60.54

Page 109   Gift of George Blumenthal, 1941   41.100.195

Page 110   Stewart S. MacDermott Fund, 1977   1977.550 a,b

Page 111   Rogers Fund, 1906   06.1046

Page 112   Rogers Fund, 1911   11.212.12

Page 113   Rogers Fund, 1920   20.192.1

Page 114   Robert Lehman Collection, 1975   1975.1.944

Page 115   Robert Lehman Collection, 1975   1975.1.945

Page 116   Bequest of Collis P. Huntington, 1900   25.110.6

Page 117   Gift of Mr. and Mrs. Charles Wrightsman, 1977   1977.1.3

Page 118   The Elisha Whittelsey Collection,
The Elisha Whittelsey Fund, 1954   54.602.1(14)

Page 119   Purchase, Mary Wetmore Shively Bequest,
in memory of her husband, Henry L. Shively, M.D., 1954   54.195

Page 120   Robert Lehman Collection, 1975   1975.1.31

Page 121   Purchase, Pfeiffer Fund, 1962   62.120.1

Page 122   The Cloisters Collection, 1968   68.174

Page 123   Purchase, Rogers and Fletcher Funds; The Vincent Astor
Foundation, The Dillon Fund, The Charles Engelhard Foundation,
Lawrence A. Fleischman, Mrs. Henry J. Heinz II, The Willard
T. C. Johnson Foundation Inc., Reliance Group Holdings Inc.,
Baron H. H. Thyssen-Bornemisza, and Mr. and Mrs. Charles
Wrightsman Gifts; Joseph Pulitzer Bequest; special funds;
and other gifts and bequests, by exchange, 1983   1983.451

Page 124   Gift of Lillian Nassau, 1976   1976.105

Page 125   Gift of Alexander Smith Cochran, 1913   13.228.33

Page 126   The Sackler Fund, 1969   69.242.10

Page 127   The Sackler Fund, 1972   1972.122c

Page 128   Gift of Francis Leonard Cater, 1958   58.584

Page 129   Fletcher Fund, 1936   36.14a–c

Page 130 and 131   Rogers Fund, 1907   07.201

Page 132   The Jules Bache Collection, 1949   49.7.52

Page 133   Bequest of Scofield Thayer, 1982   1984.433.16

Page 134   Gift of Alexander Smith Cochran, 1913   13.228.13 folio 23v

Page 135   Purchase, Louis V. Bell Fund and
The Vincent Astor Foundation Gift, 1974   1974.294.2

Page 136   Fletcher Fund, 1929   JP 1548

Page 137   Bequest of Stephen Whitney Phoenix, 1881   81.1.153

INDEX OF ARTISTS, AUTHORS, AND TITLES